MARIUS FATE
THE MODERN GAME

THE MODERN GAME

Written by Mark Sheeky.
Illustrations and graphic design by Mark Sheeky.

1st edition, published by Pentangel Books.
www.pentangel.co.uk
ISBN 978-0-9571947-7-9

Cornutopia Music
www.cornutopiamusic.com

This book can be sold
as a special edition with CD
You can order your CD
for this book from
www.marksheeky.com

THE
MODERN
GAME

Mark's Fate

THE MODERN GAME

THE MODERN GAME

THE MODERN GAME

Don't you think
that all the best beginnings...

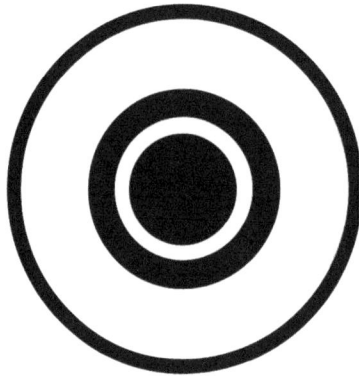

01100111
01100001
01101101
01100101

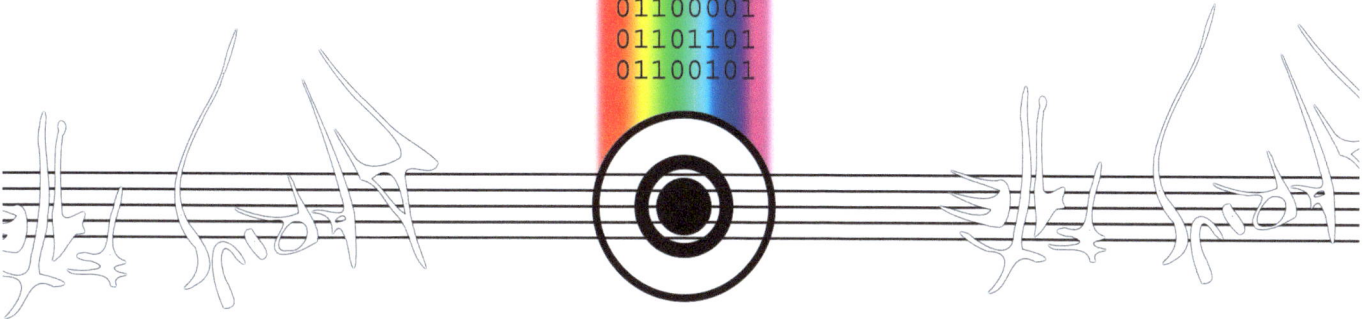

BEGINNINGS

BEYOND MARS

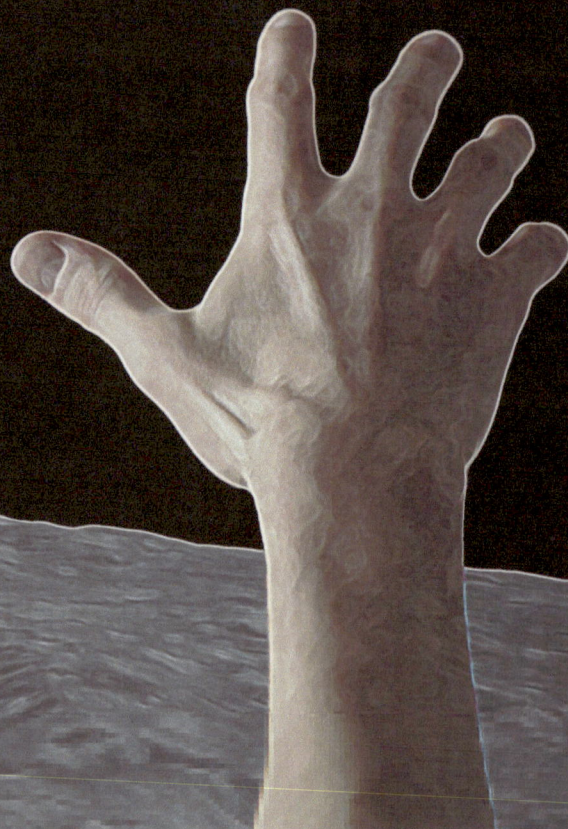

BEYOND MARS

It was cold as the Twitter-scape.
It was fake as electric vape.
There was only a sense that there could be more than this.

There was nothing about the place
but a sign called hope
close to the door,

and the sign said
watch me singing karaoke,
hear me playing my acoustic,
latest internet sensation due,

drug me, stop me feeling sad,
out here in deep space, far away,
on a planet beyond Mars.

Make a wish upon a planet.

We began to feel ill again.
It was time for a pill again.
They were given out for free so it was not hard to refuse.
To be honest they gave a certain sense of not caring at all,

makes it easier to
keep on singing karaoke,
keep on playing my acoustic,
keep on following the Facebook feed,

helps me, stops me feeling sad,
out here in space, far away,
beyond Mars.

HOUSE OF GLASS

I'm alone but I'm with my friends; I type out a message and I pretend.
Follow me to a world of things that I like,
and click like.

You can count popularity,
you can see who I like and see who likes me.
It's a game, only this game never ends,
so come and play in the room in the screen of life,
with the friends you don't know,
and me in the house of glass.

I'm a clown with a painted smile to show to a world that is in denial.
It's control and we all have bits of a string we can pull

I would like to request you as a friend...
as a friend...
friend.

You can leave,
but I must make clear,
that your work, love and friendships are all on here
you can pay to be famous if you want.
so come and play in the room in the screen of life,
with the friends you don't know,
and me in the house of glass

spend your time at the screen of life,
with your friends and pretend,
with me in the house,
with us in the house,
alone in the house,
of glass.

4

I'M ALONE

BUT I'M WITH MY FRIENDS

IT'S A GAME

6

LOOKING FOR A LOVER?

LOOKING FOR A LOVER

Welcome to the love zone...

Lookin' for a lover?
Look online.
Lookin' for a one night stand?
Lookin' for a lover?
Take your pick:
woman or a man.

Lookin' for a lover?
Look online.
Everythin' we got on show.
Lookin' for a lover?
Look all day.
It's all free to go.

Lookin' for a lover,
look all night
knowin' that they won't look back.
Come a little closer, come
into the trap.

Specify your desire...

All free...
All free...
All free love.

Lookin' for a lover?
Look online.
Everybody lookin' there.
Lookin' for a lover,
black or white;
everybody got a share.

Lookin' for a lover?
Look online.
Get it over in a blink.
Lookin' for a lover?
Sit and click.
Love at your fingertips.

Lookin' for a lover,
look all night
knowin' that they won't look back.
Come a little closer, come
into the trap.

MASCULINITY TWO

MASCULINITY TWO

You can blink at me slowly,
you can flicker your lips,
but it won't get to my,
metal heart.

You can signal me baby,
send me sex in your sips,
but it's ice in the soul,
of the dark.

Welcome to the new paradise,
what do you want to do?
Want to come and a play game with me tonight?

Masculinity two.

Welcome to the new paradise,
What do you want to do?
Want to come and a play game with me tonight?

Masculinity two.

This is what you all wanted.
This electro control.
This is love into fire,
into death.

So keep signalling baby,
I'll keep looking away,
as I drink as I die,
as I play.

THE TREES

Here in the trees of people we hide from the sound of their wooden bones that crisp and creak we hear them whisper about us their voices control us the voices we speak to, type to, at night;

they are trees.

THEY ARE TREES!

THEIR VOICES CONTROL
US THEY SHOUT
AS ONE THEY
SHOUT THE TREES
SHOUT THE TREES
OF PEOPLE.

THE TREES
OF PEOPLE
SILENCE US
MAKE US SCREAM
INSIDE
THE TREES
MAKE US
SCREAM.

HERE IN THE TREES

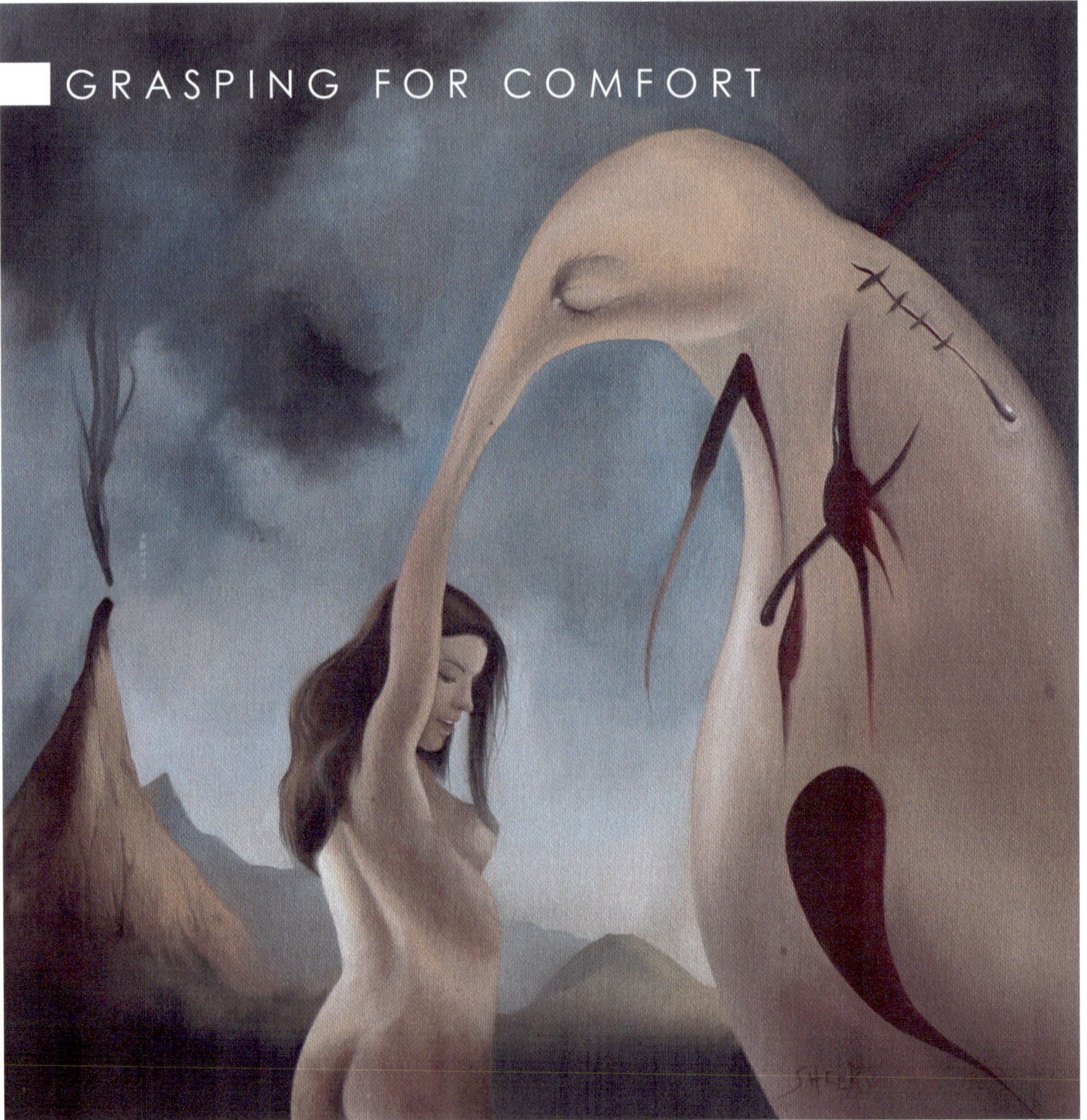

LOVE IN A HOPELESS WORLD

🔍 |

In the search box
wandering from thing to person
looking for a new attraction
for a brief dis-traction
in a dead fog
in an ice void of thought
like a lost astronaut
grasping for comfort
seeking love, love, love in a hopeless world
love, love, love in a hopeless world
love, love, love in a hopeless world
seeking love, love...

Make excuses
anything to be evasive
thinking of a god to play with
something to escape with
these are cold streets
need a beer to keep warm
I'm a sparrow in swarm
searching for comfort
seeking love, love, love in a hopeless world
love, love, love in a hopeless world
love, love, love in a hopeless world
seeking love, love...

TWO KINDS OF ANIMALS

There are two kinds of animals in this world,
the ones that are useful within this world,
and ones that are useless within in this world...

There are those that like towns like the fox and rats,
and those that avoid us like birds and bats,
but unless they can help us we put out traps...

There are those that have comforting barks and meows.
and those that we eat like the sheep and cows.
but the rest are a pest and are not allowed...

THEY MUST ALL BE OUR SLAVES!
BE OUR SLAVES OR DIE!

MESSAGE FROM CENTRAL CONTROL:
ALL HUMANS MUST REPORT TO UNIT FOUR FOR REPROGRAMMING.

WHAT KIND OF ANIMAL ARE YOU?
WHAT KIND OF ANIMAL ARE YOU?
ARE YOU USEFUL TO US?

There are two kinds of animals in this world,
the ones that are useful within this world,
and ones that are useless within in this world...

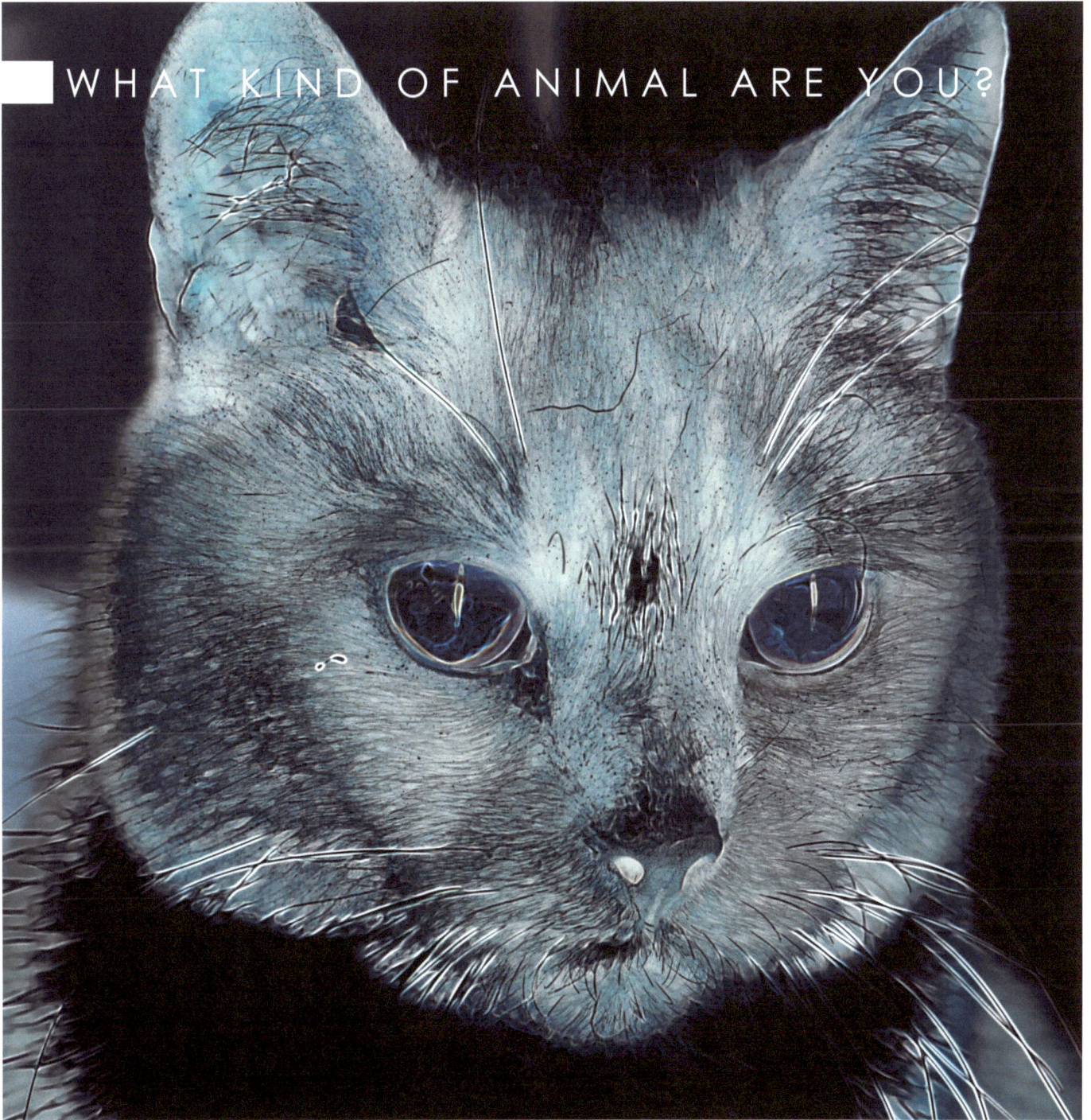

WHAT KIND OF ANIMAL ARE YOU?

ALL THE BROKEN FLOWERS

ALL THE BROKEN FLOWERS

All the broken flowers that she gave me
as Christmas presents, as birthday gifts.
She gave what she could, but had nothing.
Oh how pitiful, the anguish.

All the broken flowers that she gave me,
lined up on the window sill waiting for entropy
to eat them away, like her bones, her hair
now grey and lost, the anguish.

Eight summers since we met, five of rain.
How being downtrodden can be addictive,
and how romantic nostalgia is
hiding the awful truth in a cloud of pink scent
of flowers.

Eight summers since we met, five of rain,
and now she is gone to heaven.
How romantic nostalgia is
like a cloak of comfort for the tears.

Perhaps if I'd loved the flowers more
she wouldn't have broken.

NOTES FROM SPACE

Night rain falls
I stare in from outside
Watch the lace-wings of water die
head first cascade into deep tumble
whirls of moonlit dust
a straggle of refugees
grey pink explosions
across the plate of the earth
beings deep crushed inside
hazelnuts, bathyspheres, deep crushed
the ice rain bites
blades of water scream
and crash through
falling night.

NIGHT RAIN FALLS

COMING BACK TO EARTH

COMING BACK TO EARTH

Hello from the sea,
you look lost,
did you miss me?
I was dying.
Now I'm free.
Now I'm back to save you,
Be happy.

You look like you've been through a tough time
through the wars, on your own,
your sunken eyes and paranoia,
feel like a stranger in your home,
but it's all over now.
Yes it's all over now.
Yes it's all...

Lookin' for a lover?
Here I am.

Switch off the power to your master,
take my hand, to your heart.
The years of emptiness are over,
all it took was a god...
and a miracle!

So it's hello from the sea,
take my hand, come with me.
I was dying.
Now I'm free.
Now I'm back, for you.
Be happy.

THE STARS

I like to look at the stars light

glitter like my mind

silver ice like my mind

alone in the sea of night

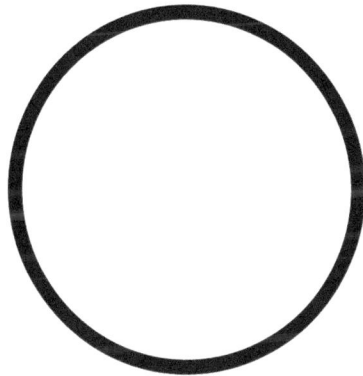

...are also endings?

CREDITS

The Modern Game
Performed by Marius Fate
Composed and produced by Mark Sheeky

Synthesized, sequenced, and produced using Prometheus v2.58 software
Featuring Microkorg, and Yamaha P105 digital piano
Microphones by RØDE
Apollo project samples courtesy of NASA
Mastered using Sony CD Architect v5.2

ILLUSTRATIONS

IT'S A GAME
The Deadly Allure of Facebook (2013)
Oil on M.D.F. panel, 336x234mm

GRASPING FOR COMFORT
Threads of Love as Comfort (2017)
Oil on canvas panel, 280x280mm

Space images courtesy of NASA

01100111
01100001
01101101
01100101

01101111
01110110
01100101
01110010